PURE
Vanilla

MORE THAN 55 DELICIOUS RECIPES

Publications International, Ltd.

Pictured on the front cover *(clockwise from top left)*: Colorful Meringue Cookies
(page 22), Ultimate Vanilla Cheesecake *(page 42)*, Vanilla Sugar Cookies *(page 32)*, and
Easy Vanilla Layer Cake *(page 48)*.

Pictured on the back cover *(clockwise from top left)*: Creamy Stuffed French Toast
(page 8), Vanilla Green Beans Amandine *(page 84)*, Carrot Cake with Vanilla Cream Cheese
Frosting *(page 44)*, Vanilla Rich Chocolate Chip Cookies *(page 38)*, and Vanilla Summertime
Slaw *(page 98)*.

ISBN-13: 978-1-68022-802-1

Library of Congress Control Number: 2016956276

Manufactured in China.

8 7 6 5 4 3 2 1

Microwave Cooking: Ovens vary in wattage. Use the cooking times as guidelines and
check for doneness before adding more time.

Preparation/Cooking Times: Preparation times are based on the approximate amount
of time required to assemble the recipe before cooking, baking, chilling or serving. These
times include preparation steps such as measuring, chopping and mixing. The fact that
some preparations and cooking can be done simultaneously is taken into account.
Preparation of optional ingredients and serving suggestions is not included.

Table of Contents

Vanilla: The Bakers' and Cooks' Best Friend

Open a bottle of McCormick® Pure Vanilla Extract. You'll smell a rich, full-bodied aroma that warms your heart. What do you taste? Our signature bourbon-vanilla flavor. It's that taste that evokes memories of a cozy kitchen, filled with food and family. Experience the difference for yourself in every bottle.

The quality of vanilla extract can vary greatly, so it's important to know where your vanilla comes from.

Vanilla extract actually comes from a flower—the fragrant orchid. The orchids grow on plants that take three years to fully mature, which then produce long, green bean pods annually. Each orchid is hand pollinated on the day it blooms by farmers we have sourced from for generations. By traveling to the best vanilla growing regions each year, we can ensure crop quality of the most premium vanilla beans available.

The art of making vanilla extract is a lesson in patience. But the wait is worth it. We batch blend beans from Madagascar and other premium growing regions to achieve high-quality pure vanilla extract year after year. McCormick sensory scientists conduct a series of tests specific to delivering our distinctive bourbony, vanilla flavor. And our pure vanilla extract is non-GMO, free of corn syrup and naturally gluten-free. Because when you start with flavor this pure, you don't need artificial anything.

Put pure flavor to practice with this special collection of McCormick recipes. Indulge in delectable vanilla desserts. Cozy up with vanilla-infused eggnog. Impress overnight guests with vanilla-inspired breakfast treats. And wow at your next family dinner with savory side dishes that use the extract in unexpected and creative ways.

From date night to holidays and every day in between, vanilla is the bakers' and cooks' best friend. However you choose to use this beloved baking staple, vanilla always brings you home.

BOUNTIFUL
Breakfasts
& Brunches

Creamy Stuffed French Toast

PREP TIME: 15 minutes | **COOK TIME:** 10 minutes

MAKES 4 SERVINGS

1 package (8 ounces) whipped cream cheese
1 tablespoon packed brown sugar
1 loaf challah *or* brioche bread, cut into 8 slices
5 eggs
1 cup milk
1 teaspoon **McCormick® Ground Cinnamon**
1 teaspoon **McCormick® Pure Vanilla Extract**
1 tablespoon butter

MIX cream cheese and brown sugar in small bowl until well blended. Spread 2 tablespoons cream cheese mixture on *each* of 4 slices of bread. Press the other 4 slices of bread on top to form 4 sandwiches.

BEAT eggs with wire whisk in 13×9-inch baking dish. Stir in milk, cinnamon and vanilla until well blended. Dip sandwiches in egg mixture, soaking for 2 minutes on each side.

MELT butter in large nonstick skillet or griddle on medium-low heat. Place sandwiches in skillet. Cook 4 to 5 minutes per side or until golden brown. Serve with maple syrup, if desired.

Flavor the Filling:

To create flavored filling variations, stir the following extract into the cream cheese mixture until well blended:

Creamy Maple Stuffed French Toast: Add 2 teaspoons **McCormick® Maple Extract**.

Creamy Coconut Stuffed French Toast: Add 1 teaspoon **McCormick® Coconut Extract**.

Creamy Rum Stuffed French Toast: Add 1 teaspoon **McCormick® Rum Extract**.

Creamy Orange Stuffed French Toast: Add 1 teaspoon **McCormick® Pure Orange Extract**.

Vanilla Rich Chocolate Chip Muffins

PREP TIME: 15 minutes | **COOK TIME:** 25 minutes

MAKES 12 SERVINGS

2 cups flour	¼ cup milk
⅔ cup sugar	¼ cup vegetable oil
1½ teaspoons baking powder	1 egg, lightly beaten
½ teaspoon baking soda	1 tablespoon **McCormick®** **Pure Vanilla Extract**
¼ teaspoon salt	
1 cup sour cream	1 cup semi-sweet chocolate chips

PREHEAT oven to 400°F. Lightly grease 12 muffin cups or line with paper baking cups. Set aside.

MIX flour, sugar, baking powder, baking soda and salt in large bowl. Mix sour cream, milk, oil, egg and vanilla in medium bowl. Add to flour mixture; stir just until dry ingredients are moistened. (Batter will be thick and slightly lumpy.) Gently stir in chocolate chips.

SPOON batter into prepared muffin cups, filling each cup ⅔ full.

BAKE 20 to 25 minutes or until toothpick inserted in center of muffins comes out clean. Serve warm.

Mini Dutch Boy Pancakes

PREP TIME: 10 minutes | **COOK TIME:** 16 minutes

MAKES 6 SERVINGS

Pancakes

- ½ cup flour
- ½ cup milk
- 3 eggs
- 2 tablespoons sugar
- 2 teaspoons **McCormick® Pure Vanilla Extract**
- ¼ teaspoon salt

Blueberry-Lemon Sauce

- 2 tablespoons sugar
- 1 teaspoon cornstarch
- 1 cup blueberries
- 3 tablespoons water
- ¼ teaspoon **McCormick® Pure Lemon Extract**

PREHEAT oven to 400°F. For the Pancakes, spray 12-cup muffin pan with no stick cooking spray. Set aside. Place all ingredients in blender container; cover. Blend on medium speed until smooth. Pour evenly into prepared muffin pan.

BAKE 13 to 16 minutes or until edges of pancakes are golden brown. Cool on wire rack 2 minutes.

FOR the Blueberry-Lemon Sauce, mix sugar and cornstarch in small saucepan. Add blueberries, water and lemon extract. Bring to boil on medium heat, stirring constantly. Boil 1 minute. Spoon sauce into center of each pancake. Sprinkle with confectioners' sugar, if desired. Serve immediately.

Very Vanilla Fruit Salad

🕐 **PREP TIME:** 15 minutes

MAKES 10 SERVINGS

2   cups strawberries, halved

1   cup blueberries

1   cup fresh or canned
     pineapple chunks

1   cup cantaloupe chunks

2   kiwis, peeled and sliced

2   teaspoons **McCormick®
     Pure Vanilla Extract**

MIX fruit and vanilla in large bowl. Cover.

REFRIGERATE 1 hour or until ready to serve.

Test Kitchen Tip: To enhance the sweetness of any unripe fruit, stir confectioners' sugar, 1 tablespoon at a time, into fruit salad until desired sweetness is reached.

Vanilla Pound Cake

PREP TIME: 15 minutes | **COOK TIME:** 1 hour 5 minutes

MAKES 12 SERVINGS

2 cups flour
1 teaspoon baking powder
¼ teaspoon salt
⅛ teaspoon **McCormick® Ground Nutmeg**

1 cup (2 sticks) butter, softened
1¼ cups sugar
4 eggs
5 teaspoons **McCormick® Pure Vanilla Extract**

PREHEAT oven to 325°F. Mix flour, baking powder, salt and nutmeg in medium bowl. Set aside.

BEAT butter and sugar in large bowl with electric mixer on medium speed 5 minutes or until light and fluffy. Beat in eggs, 1 at a time. Gradually beat in ½ of flour mixture. Mix in vanilla and remaining flour mixture. Pour batter into greased and floured 9×5×3-inch loaf pan.

BAKE 60 to 65 minutes or until toothpick inserted in center comes out clean. Cool on wire rack.

Overnight French Toast

🕐 **PREP TIME:** 15 minutes | **COOK TIME:** 25 minutes

MAKES 8 SERVINGS

1 loaf Italian bread, cut into 8 (1-inch-thick) slices

5 eggs, beaten

¾ cup milk

1 tablespoon **McCormick® Pure Vanilla Extract**

¼ cup plus 2 tablespoons granulated sugar, divided

¼ teaspoon baking powder

1 pound strawberries, halved

4 ripe bananas, sliced

1 teaspoon **McCormick® Cinnamon Sugar**

PLACE bread in single layer in large baking dish. Mix eggs, milk, vanilla, 2 tablespoons granulated sugar and baking powder in medium bowl. Pour over bread to soak; turn to coat well. Cover. Refrigerate 4 hours or overnight.

PREHEAT oven to 450°F. Mix strawberries, bananas and remaining granulated sugar in 13×9-inch baking dish. Top with soaked bread slices. Sprinkle with cinnamon sugar.

BAKE 20 to 25 minutes or until golden brown. Let stand 5 minutes before serving.

Variation:

Overnight Apple French Toast: Prepare and refrigerate bread slices as directed. Substitute 4 medium apples, peeled, cored and thinly sliced (about 4 cups) for the strawberries and bananas. Toss apples with 1 cup granulated sugar and 1 teaspoon **McCormick® Ground Cinnamon** in baking dish. Top with soaked bread slices. Sprinkle with cinnamon sugar. Cover with foil. Bake in preheated 375°F oven 30 minutes. Remove foil and bake 10 to 15 minutes longer or until apples are tender.

Maple Banana Bread Pancakes

⏱ PREP TIME: 10 minutes | **COOK TIME:** 12 minutes

MAKES 3 SERVINGS

2 large ripe bananas

2 eggs

2 tablespoons packed brown sugar

2 tablespoons melted butter

1 tablespoon **McCormick® Maple Extract**

2 teaspoons **McCormick® Pure Vanilla Extract**

1 teaspoon **McCormick® Ground Cinnamon**

¾ cup flour

2 teaspoons baking powder

MASH bananas with potato masher in large bowl. Add eggs, brown sugar, butter, maple extract, vanilla and cinnamon; mix well. Add flour and baking powder; mix until well blended.

PREHEAT lightly greased griddle or skillet over medium heat. Pour scant ¼ cup batter onto griddle. Cook 1 to 2 minutes per side or until golden brown, turning when pancakes begin to bubble.

Test Kitchen Tip: If bananas are not ripe, bake on foil-lined pan at 300°F for 40 minutes. Cool, then peel and mash bananas.

Serving Suggestion: Serve pancakes with additional sliced bananas, chopped walnuts and maple syrup.

CREATIVE
Cookies & Snacks

Colorful Meringue Cookies

PREP TIME: 10 minutes | **COOK TIME:** 45 minutes

MAKES 6 DOZEN COOKIES

4 egg whites, at room temperature

½ teaspoon **McCormick® Cream of Tartar**

1 cup sugar

1 teaspoon **McCormick® Pure Vanilla Extract**

25 drops **McCormick® Assorted NEON! Food Colors & Egg Dye**

PREHEAT oven to 225°F.

BEAT egg whites in large bowl with electric mixer on medium speed until frothy. (If using a freestanding mixer, use wire whisk attachment.) Add cream of tartar; beat until soft peaks form. Increase speed to medium-high. Add sugar, 1 tablespoon at a time, beating until sugar is dissolved and stiff peaks form. Beat in extract and food color until well blended. Gently stir in chips, if desired.

DROP by rounded measuring teaspoonfuls about 1 inch apart onto 2 large foil-lined baking sheets sprayed with no stick cooking spray.

BAKE both sheets of meringues at the same time 45 minutes. Turn oven off. Let meringues stand in oven 1 hour or until completely cooled.

Test Kitchen Tips:

• Make sure beater and mixing bowl are spotlessly clean. Any grease in the mixture will deflate meringue.

• Do not make meringues during humid weather. Moisture will prevent egg whites from forming stiff peaks.

• To make different shapes of meringue, spoon meringue mixture into large resealable plastic bag. Snip off a corner of the bag and gently squeeze to pipe meringue onto baking sheets. Pipe into various shapes, such as hearts, "kisses," letters, numbers, etc.

• Try also with ½ teaspoon *each* **McCormick® Pure Vanilla Extract** and **McCormick® Pure Mint Extract**.

• Add 1 cup mini chocolate chips, if desired.

Red Velvet Crinkle Cookies

🕐 **PREP TIME:** 20 minutes | **COOK TIME:** 12 minutes

MAKES 4 DOZEN COOKIES

1⅔ cups flour	2 eggs
⅓ cup unsweetened cocoa powder	1½ teaspoons **McCormick® Red Food Color**
1½ teaspoons baking powder	1 teaspoon **McCormick® Pure Vanilla Extract**
¼ teaspoon salt	½ cup confectioners' sugar
½ cup (1 stick) butter, softened	
1¼ cups granulated sugar	

MIX flour, cocoa powder, baking powder and salt in medium bowl. Set aside. Beat butter and granulated sugar in large bowl with electric mixer on medium speed until light and fluffy. Add eggs, food color and vanilla; mix well. Gradually beat in flour mixture on low speed until well mixed. Refrigerate 4 hours.

PREHEAT oven to 350°F. Shape dough into 1-inch balls. Roll in confectioners' sugar to completely coat. Place 2 inches apart onto baking sheets sprayed with no stick cooking spray.

BAKE 10 to 12 minutes or until cookies are puffed. Cool on baking sheets 2 minutes. Remove to wire racks; cool completely.

Test Kitchen Tip: Add 1 cup semi-sweet chocolate chips or miniature chocolate chips to the dough.

Variation: Prepare as directed, adding 1 teaspoon **McCormick® Raspberry Extract**.

Chocolate Chip Cookie Biscotti with White Chocolate Dipping Sauce

🕐 **PREP TIME:** 20 minutes | **COOK TIME:** 45 minutes

MAKES 16 SERVINGS

Biscotti

2½ cups flour

1 cup firmly packed brown sugar

¼ cup instant nonfat dry milk

2 teaspoons baking powder

¼ teaspoon salt

3 eggs

1 teaspoon **McCormick® Pure Vanilla Extract**

1 cup miniature chocolate chips

Dipping Sauce

2¼ cups half-and-half

8 ounces white chocolate chips

2 teaspoons **McCormick® Pure Vanilla Extract**

PREHEAT oven to 350°F. For the Biscotti, mix flour, brown sugar, dry milk, baking powder and salt in large bowl with electric mixer on low speed until well blended. Mix eggs and vanilla in medium bowl until well blended. Gradually add to flour mixture, beating on low speed until well mixed. Stir in chocolate chips.

DIVIDE dough in half. Shape each half into a 12-inch-long log. Transfer logs to parchment paper-lined baking sheet. Flatten logs to 1-inch thickness.

BAKE 20 to 25 minutes or until slightly risen and firm to touch. Cool logs on wire rack 10 minutes or until cool enough to handle. Transfer to cutting board. Using a sharp serrated knife, cut logs diagonally into ¾-inch-thick slices. Place slices, cut sides down, in single layer on parchment paper-lined baking sheets.

BAKE 10 to 15 minutes or until crisp and golden, turning biscotti over halfway through cook time. Remove biscotti to wire racks; cool completely.

FOR the Dipping Sauce, place all ingredients in medium saucepan on medium heat. Simmer 5 minutes or until heated through, stirring constantly. Serve with biscotti.

Very Vanilla Marshmallows

🕐 **PREP TIME:** 40 minutes

MAKES 24 SERVINGS

1½ cups confectioners' sugar, divided

1 cup cold water, divided

2 cups granulated sugar

½ cup light corn syrup

2 envelopes (¼ ounce *each*) unflavored gelatin

1 tablespoon **McCormick® Pure Vanilla Extract**

SPRAY 9-inch square baking dish with no stick cooking spray then coat with some of the confectioners' sugar. Set aside. Microwave ½ cup of the water, granulated sugar and corn syrup in medium microwavable bowl on HIGH 7 minutes. Stir to dissolve sugar. Microwave on HIGH 5 minutes longer. (Mixture will have a slight yellow tint.) Carefully remove hot bowl from microwave.

PLACE remaining ½ cup water in mixer bowl. Sprinkle with gelatin. Let stand 5 minutes. Gradually beat in hot syrup mixture with whisk attachment on medium-low speed. Beat 8 minutes. Increase speed to medium-high. Beat 10 to 12 minutes longer or until mixture is fluffy, shiny and at least tripled in volume. Beat in vanilla.

SPREAD marshmallow mixture in prepared pan. Smooth top with a spatula. Sift about 2 tablespoons of the confectioners' sugar over top. Let stand at room temperature overnight or refrigerate at least 3 hours.

PLACE remaining confectioners' sugar in large bowl. Cut marshmallows into 1½-inch squares. Add marshmallows in batches to confectioners' sugar; toss to coat well. Shake off excess. Store marshmallows in airtight container at room temperature up to 3 days.

Test Kitchen Tips:

• Microwave syrup mixture in a 4-cup glass measuring cup for easy pouring.

• Microwave ovens vary; adjust cooking times as needed. Cooking times are based on a 1200-watt microwave oven.

Stovetop Directions: Cook syrup mixture in a small heavy saucepan on medium heat until mixture just begins to color and reaches 240°F on a candy thermometer. Continue as directed.

Browned Butter Cinnamon Shortbread Cookies

PREP TIME: 20 minutes | **COOK TIME:** 1 hour

MAKES 16 SERVINGS

1 cup (2 sticks) butter, cut into chunks	½ cup granulated sugar
1¾ cups flour	¼ cup firmly packed light brown sugar
¼ cup cornstarch	1 tablespoon **McCormick® Pure Vanilla Extract**
1½ teaspoons **McCormick® Ground Cinnamon**, divided	8 ounces semi-sweet chocolate
¼ teaspoon salt	

MELT butter in medium heavy-bottomed saucepan on medium heat. Cook 3 to 4 minutes or until butter forms browned specks on bottom of pan, stirring occasionally. Pour butter into large bowl. Cool slightly. Refrigerate 1 hour or until butter returns to the consistency of room temperature butter.

LINE 9-inch square baking pan with foil. Spray with no stick cooking spray. Mix flour, cornstarch, ½ teaspoon of the cinnamon and salt in medium bowl. Set aside. Add sugars and vanilla to browned butter; beat with electric mixer on medium speed until light and fluffy, scraping sides occasionally. Gradually beat in flour mixture on low speed until well mixed. Press dough evenly in prepared pan.

BAKE in preheated 300°F oven 55 to 60 minutes or until center is firm and edges are lightly browned. Immediately, cut shortbread into 4 squares then cut each square crosswise into 4 triangles. While still warm but not hot, remove shortbread from pan to wire rack to cool.

MELT chocolate as directed on package. Stir in remaining 1 teaspoon cinnamon. Drizzle chocolate over shortbread triangles. Let stand on wax paper-lined tray until chocolate is set.

Vanilla Sugar Cookies

🕐 **PREP TIME:** 20 minutes | **COOK TIME:** 6 minutes

MAKES 4½ DOZEN COOKIES

2¾ cups flour

2 teaspoons **McCormick® Cream of Tartar**

1 teaspoon baking soda

½ teaspoon salt

1½ cups sugar

1 cup (2 sticks) butter, softened

2 eggs

2 teaspoons **McCormick® Pure Vanilla Extract**

Additional sugar, for rolling*

*Can substitute with Colored Sugar (recipe follows).

MIX flour, cream of tartar, baking soda and salt in large bowl. Set aside. Beat sugar and butter in large bowl with electric mixer on medium speed until light and fluffy. Add eggs and vanilla; mix well. Gradually beat in flour mixture on low speed until well mixed.

REFRIGERATE dough 2 hours or until firm.

PREHEAT oven to 400°F. Shape dough into 1-inch balls. Roll in additional sugar or Colored Sugar. Place 2 inches apart on baking sheets.

BAKE 6 to 8 minutes or until lightly browned. Cool on baking sheets 1 minute. Remove to wire racks; cool completely.

Flavor Variations: Add 2 teaspoons **McCormick® Pure Almond Flavor** or **Pure Lemon Extract**.

Colored Sugar: Place ½ cup granulated or sanding sugar in resealable plastic bag. Add 5 drops of **McCormick® Assorted Food Colors and Egg Dye** or **McCormick® Assorted NEON! Food Colors and Egg Dye**. Add additional food color, a drop or two at a time, if more intense color is desired. Seal bag and knead sugar until the color is evenly distributed. Spread in a thin layer on a baking sheet and break up any large lumps. Allow to dry thoroughly, about 15 to 20 minutes. Sift or press through sieve to return sugar to its original texture, if needed.

Cinnamon Vanilla Glazed Walnuts

🕐 **PREP TIME:** 5 minutes | **COOK TIME:** 1 hour

MAKES 10 SERVINGS

¼ cup sugar	¼ teaspoon salt
1½ teaspoons **McCormick®** **Ground Cinnamon**	1 egg white
	1 tablespoon **McCormick®** **Pure Vanilla Extract**
⅛ teaspoon **McCormick®** **Ground Red Pepper**	2 cups walnut halves

PREHEAT oven to 250°F. Mix sugar, cinnamon, red pepper and salt in small bowl. Set aside.

BEAT egg white and vanilla in medium bowl until foamy. Add walnuts; toss to coat. Add spice mixture; toss to coat nuts evenly. Spread nuts in single layer on greased baking sheet.

BAKE 1 hour, stirring nuts after 30 minutes. Cool slightly and break apart. Cool completely and store in airtight container up to 2 weeks.

Vanilla White Chocolate Pistachio Fudge

🕐 **PREP TIME:** 10 minutes

MAKES 18 SERVINGS

12   ounces white chocolate, coarsely chopped

¾   cup sweetened condensed milk

1   cup shelled salted pistachios

¼   cup chopped dried cranberries*

1   tablespoon **McCormick® Pure Vanilla Extract**

Can substitute ¼ cup chopped dried cherries.

PLACE white chocolate in large microwavable bowl. Add sweetened condensed milk; mix well. Microwave on HIGH 2 to 3 minutes or until chocolate is almost melted, stirring after every minute. Stir until chocolate is completely melted. Stir in pistachios, cranberries and vanilla.

POUR chocolate mixture into foil-lined 8-inch-square baking pan.

REFRIGERATE 2 hours or until fudge is set. Use foil to lift out of pan onto cutting board. Cut into 36 pieces. Store in tightly covered container at cool room temperature.

Pecan Cookie Balls

🕐 **PREP TIME:** 20 minutes | **COOK TIME:** 15 minutes

MAKES 4 DOZEN COOKIES

- 1 cup (2 sticks) butter, softened
- 2½ cups confectioners' sugar, divided
- 2 teaspoons **McCormick® Pure Vanilla Extract**
- ½ teaspoon **McCormick® Ground Nutmeg**
- ⅛ teaspoon salt
- 2 cups flour
- 2 cups finely chopped pecans

PREHEAT oven to 350°F. Beat butter in large bowl with electric mixer on medium speed until light and fluffy. Add ½ cup of the confectioners' sugar, vanilla, nutmeg and salt; beat until well blended. Stir in flour and pecans.

SHAPE into 1-inch balls. Place 1 inch apart on ungreased baking sheets.

BAKE 15 minutes. Remove from baking sheets. Immediately roll hot cookies in remaining 2 cups sugar. Place sugared cookies on wire racks to cool. When cool, roll again in sugar.

Variation:

Cinnamon Pecan Cookie Balls: Add ½ teaspoon **McCormick® Ground Cinnamon** to the cookie dough, adding with the nutmeg. Add ½ teaspoon cinnamon to the 2 cups confectioners' sugar for rolling.

Vanilla Rich Chocolate Chip Cookies

PREP TIME: 15 minutes | **COOK TIME:** 8 minutes

MAKES 5 DOZEN COOKIES

3¼	cups flour	2	eggs
1	teaspoon baking soda	4	teaspoons **McCormick® Pure Vanilla Extract**
¾	teaspoon salt	1	package (12 ounces) semi-sweet chocolate chips
1⅓	cups butter, softened		
1¼	cups granulated sugar	1	cup chopped walnuts
1	cup firmly packed light brown sugar		

PREHEAT oven to 375°F. Mix flour, baking soda and salt in medium bowl. Set aside. Beat butter and sugars in large bowl with electric mixer on medium speed until light and fluffy. Add eggs and vanilla; mix well. Gradually beat in flour mixture on low speed until well mixed. Stir in chocolate chips and walnuts.

DROP by rounded tablespoons about 2 inches apart onto ungreased baking sheets.

BAKE 8 to 10 minutes or until lightly browned. Cool on baking sheets 1 minute. Remove to wire racks; cool completely.

Variations:

Cranberry, Macadamia & White Chocolate Chip Cookies: Add 1 teaspoon **McCormick® Ground Cinnamon** with the flour. Use 1 cup *each* dried cranberries, chopped toasted macadamia nuts and white chocolate chips in place of the semi-sweet chocolate chips and walnuts. Makes 6 dozen.

Coconut, Raisin & Pecan Cookies: Add 1 teaspoon **McCormick® Ground Cinnamon** with the flour. Use 1 cup *each* flaked coconut, raisins and chopped toasted pecans in place of the semi-sweet chocolate chips and walnuts. Makes 5 dozen.

Coconut Almond Chocolate Chip Cookies: Add 1 teaspoon **McCormick® Pure Almond Extract**. Use 1 cup *each* flaked coconut, toasted slivered almonds and semi-sweet chocolate chips in place of the 2 cups semi-sweet chocolate chips and walnuts. Makes 5 dozen.

CLASSY
Cakes &
Cheesecakes

Ultimate Vanilla Cheesecake

PREP TIME: 15 minutes | **COOK TIME:** 50 minutes

MAKES 12 SERVINGS

Vanilla Wafer Crust

- 50 vanilla wafers, finely crushed (2 cups)
- ⅓ cup butter, melted
- ¼ cup sugar
- 1 teaspoon **McCormick® Pure Vanilla Extract**

Cheesecake Filling

- 3 packages (8 ounces *each*) cream cheese, softened
- 1 cup sugar
- 4 eggs
- 1 cup sour cream
- 1 tablespoon **McCormick® Pure Vanilla Extract**

PREHEAT oven to 325°F. For the Vanilla Wafer Crust, mix vanilla wafer crumbs, butter, sugar and vanilla in medium bowl until well blended. Press evenly into bottom and 2 inches up sides of 9-inch springform pan. Set aside.

FOR the Cheesecake Filling, beat cream cheese and sugar in large bowl with electric mixer on high speed until well blended. Add eggs, 1 at a time, mixing on low speed after each addition just until blended. Add sour cream and vanilla; mix well. Pour into prepared crust.

BAKE 50 minutes or until center is almost set. Turn off oven. Leave cheesecake in oven 2 hours or until cooled. Remove from oven.

REFRIGERATE 4 hours or overnight. Run small knife around sides of pan to loosen crust; remove sides of pan. Store leftover cheesecake in refrigerator.

Carrot Cake with Vanilla Cream Cheese Frosting

PREP TIME: 10 minutes | **COOK TIME:** 35 minutes

MAKES 16 SERVINGS

Carrot Cake

- 2 cups flour
- 2 cups granulated sugar
- 2 teaspoons baking powder
- 2 teaspoons **McCormick® Ground Cinnamon**
- ½ teaspoon **McCormick® Ground Nutmeg**
- ½ teaspoon salt
- 1¼ cups vegetable oil
- 4 eggs, lightly beaten
- 1 tablespoon **McCormick® Pure Vanilla Extract**
- 3 cups shredded carrots

Vanilla Cream Cheese Frosting

- 1 package (8 ounces) cream cheese, softened
- ½ cup (1 stick) butter, softened
- 1 teaspoon **McCormick® Pure Vanilla Extract**
- 1 package (16 ounces) confectioners' sugar

Chopped pecans (optional)

PREHEAT oven to 350°F. For the Cake, mix flour, granulated sugar, baking powder, cinnamon, nutmeg and salt in large bowl. Add oil, eggs and vanilla; mix well. Add carrots; mix until well blended. Pour batter into 2 (9-inch) greased and floured round cake pans.

BAKE 30 to 35 minutes or until toothpick inserted in centers comes out clean. Cool in pans on wire rack.

FOR the Vanilla Cream Cheese Frosting, beat cream cheese, butter and vanilla in large bowl with electric mixer on medium speed until well blended. Gradually add confectioners' sugar, beating well after each addition. Frost cooled cake with Vanilla Cream Cheese Frosting. Garnish as desired.

Vanilla Pistachio Cake with Raspberry Buttercream

🕐 **PREP TIME:** 25 minutes | **COOK TIME:** 30 minutes

MAKES 16 SERVINGS

Vanilla Pistachio Cake

1½ cups shelled salted pistachios, divided

1 package (2-layer size) yellow cake mix

1 egg

1 tablespoon **McCormick® Pure Vanilla Extract**

Raspberry Buttercream

1 cup (2 sticks) butter, softened

1 tablespoon **McCormick® Raspberry Extract**

1 package (16 ounces) confectioners' sugar

2 tablespoons milk

Fresh raspberries (optional)

PLACE 1 cup of the pistachios in food processor or clean coffee grinder; cover. Pulse until finely ground. Prepare cake mix as directed on package, adding 1 additional egg, ground pistachios and vanilla.

BAKE as directed in 2 (9-inch) round cake pans. Cool in pans 10 minutes. Remove from pans; cool completely on wire racks.

FOR the Raspberry Buttercream, beat butter and raspberry flavor in large bowl until light and fluffy. Gradually add confectioners' sugar, beating well after each addition and scraping sides and bottom of bowl frequently. Add milk; beat until light and fluffy. If frosting is too thick to spread, gradually beat in additional milk. Fill and frost cooled cake with Raspberry Buttercream. Garnish with remaining ½ cup pistachios and raspberries, if desired.

Easy Vanilla Layer Cake

1 package (2-layer size) white cake mix

3 eggs

1½ cups milk

2 tablespoons vegetable oil

4 teaspoons **McCormick® Pure Vanilla Extract**

Whipped Vanilla Buttercream Frosting (recipe follows)

PREHEAT oven to 350°F. Mix cake mix, eggs, milk, oil and vanilla in large bowl with electric mixer on low speed 1 minute. Beat on medium speed 2 minutes. Pour into 2 greased and floured 9-inch round baking pans.

BAKE as directed on package. Cool on wire racks.

PLACE cake layer on serving plate. Spread with about ½ cup of Whipped Vanilla Buttercream Frosting. Top with remaining cake layer. Frost top and sides of cake with remaining frosting. Garnish as desired.

Whipped Vanilla Buttercream Frosting

1 cup (2 sticks) butter, softened

2 teaspoons **McCormick® Pure Vanilla Extract**

1 package (16 ounces) confectioners' sugar, sifted

2 tablespoons milk

BEAT butter in large bowl with electric mixer on medium speed until light and fluffy. Add vanilla; mix well.

GRADUALLY beat in confectioners' sugar, beating until well blended after each addition, frequently scraping sides and bottom of bowl. Add milk; beat until light and fluffy. If frosting is too thick to spread, gradually beat in additional milk. Store in refrigerator up to 2 weeks. Rewhip before using.

Easy Mini Cheesecakes

⏱ **PREP TIME:** 15 minutes | **COOK TIME:** 24 minutes

MAKES 12 SERVINGS

2 packages (8 ounces *each*) cream cheese, softened

⅔ cup sugar

2 eggs

2 teaspoons **McCormick® Pure Vanilla Extract**

½ teaspoon **McCormick® Pure Almond Extract**

12 vanilla wafers

PREHEAT oven to 325°F. Beat cream cheese and sugar in large bowl with electric mixer on medium speed until light and fluffy. Add eggs and extracts; beat well.

LINE 12 muffin cups with paper baking cups. Place a wafer in bottom of each muffin cup. Spoon batter into each cup, filling each ⅔ full.

BAKE 22 to 24 minutes or until centers are almost set. Cool in pan on wire rack. (Mini cheesecakes will deflate in center upon cooling.)

REFRIGERATE 4 hours or overnight. Garnish as desired.

Topping Suggestions: Top with lemon curd, fresh fruit or melted chocolate.

Ultimate Chocolate Cake

🕐 **PREP TIME:** 45 minutes | **COOK TIME:** 30 minutes

MAKES 16 SERVINGS

Chocolate Cake

- 1 cup boiling water
- ¾ cup unsweetened cocoa powder
- 3 ounces semi-sweet chocolate, coarsely chopped
- 1 tablespoon **McCormick® Pure Vanilla Extract**
- 2½ cups flour
- 1¾ teaspoons baking soda
- 1 teaspoon baking powder
- ¼ teaspoon salt
- 1 cup (2 sticks) butter, softened
- 1⅓ cups granulated sugar
- ½ cup firmly packed brown sugar
- 4 eggs
- ¾ cup buttermilk

Chocolate Fudge Frosting

- 2¼ cups confectioners' sugar
- ¼ cup unsweetened cocoa powder
- ¼ teaspoon **McCormick® Ground Cinnamon**
- 6 ounces (¾ package) cream cheese, softened
- ¾ cup (1½ sticks) butter, softened
- 8 ounces semi-sweet chocolate, melted and cooled slightly
- 1 tablespoon **McCormick® Pure Vanilla Extract**

PREHEAT oven to 350°F. Grease and flour 2 (9-inch) round cake pans. Mix boiling water and cocoa powder in medium bowl with wire whisk until well blended. Add chopped chocolate; mix well. Let stand 20 minutes or until cooled; stirring occasionally. Stir in vanilla. Set aside. Mix flour, baking soda, baking powder and salt in medium bowl. Set aside.

BEAT butter and sugars in large bowl with electric mixer on medium speed until light and fluffy. Beat in eggs, 1 at a time. Beat in cocoa powder mixture until well blended. Alternately beat in flour mixture and buttermilk on low speed until just blended. Pour batter into prepared pans.

BAKE 25 to 30 minutes or until toothpick inserted in center comes out clean. Cool in pan 10 minutes. Remove from pans; cool completely on wire rack.

FOR the Chocolate Fudge Frosting, mix confectioners' sugar, cocoa powder and cinnamon in medium bowl until well blended. Set aside. Beat cream cheese and butter in large bowl with electric mixer on medium speed until smooth. Gradually beat in cocoa mixture on low speed until well blended. Gradually beat in melted chocolate then vanilla until well blended. Fill and frost cake with Frosting.

Storage Tip: Store frosted cake in refrigerator. Let stand at room temperature 1 hour before serving.

Vanilla Raspberry Cheesecake Bars

PREP TIME: 15 minutes | **COOK TIME:** 45 minutes

MAKES 24 SERVINGS

- 1½ cups graham cracker crumbs
- ⅓ cup butter, melted
- 2 tablespoons plus 1 cup sugar, divided
- ½ teaspoon **McCormick® Ground Ginger**
- 4 packages (8 ounces *each*) cream cheese, softened
- 2 tablespoons flour
- 1 tablespoon **McCormick® Pure Vanilla Extract**
- 4 eggs
- ¼ cup raspberry preserves, stirred to soften

PREHEAT oven to 350°F. In small bowl, mix graham cracker crumbs, butter, 2 tablespoons sugar and ginger. Press firmly onto bottom of foil-lined 13×9-inch baking pan. Refrigerate until ready to use.

BEAT cream cheese and 1 cup sugar in large bowl with electric mixer on medium speed until well blended. Add flour and vanilla; mix well. Add eggs, 1 at a time, beating on low speed after each addition just until blended. Pour over crust. Gently drop small spoonfuls of preserves over batter. Cut through batter several times with knife for marble effect.

BAKE 40 to 45 minutes or until center is almost set. Cool completely on wire rack.

REFRIGERATE 4 hours or overnight. Lift out of pan onto cutting board. Cut into bars. Garnish as desired. Store leftover bars in refrigerator.

Vanilla White Cake with Whipped Vanilla Buttercream

PREP TIME: 20 minutes | **COOK TIME:** 30 minutes

MAKES 16 SERVINGS

Vanilla White Cake

2 cups granulated sugar

1 cup sour cream

½ cup (1 stick) butter, melted

6 egg whites

1 tablespoon **McCormick® Pure Vanilla Extract**

3 cups flour

1 tablespoon baking powder

Whipped Vanilla Buttercream

1 cup (2 sticks) butter, softened

2 teaspoons **McCormick® Pure Vanilla Extract**

1 package (16 ounces) confectioners' sugar

2 tablespoons milk

PREHEAT oven to 350°F. For the Cake, beat all ingredients in large bowl with electric mixer on low speed until mixed. Beat on medium speed 2 minutes or until well blended, scraping sides of bowl occasionally. Pour batter evenly into 2 (9-inch) round cake pans sprayed with no stick cooking spray.

BAKE 25 to 29 minutes or until toothpick inserted in center comes out clean. Cool in pans 10 minutes. Remove from pans; cool completely on wire racks.

FOR the Whipped Vanilla Buttercream, beat butter and vanilla in large bowl until light and fluffy. Gradually add confectioners' sugar, beating well after each addition and scraping sides and bottom of bowl frequently. Add milk; beat until light and fluffy. If frosting is too thick to spread, gradually beat in additional milk. Fill and frost cooled cake with Buttercream.

Variation:

Vanilla White Cupcakes: Spoon batter into 24 paper-lined muffin cups. Bake in preheated 350°F oven 15 to 17 minutes or until toothpick inserted into cupcake comes out clean. Cool in pans on wire rack 5 minutes. Remove from pans; cool completely. Frost cooled cupcakes with Whipped Vanilla Buttercream. Makes 24 servings.

Vanilla Hot Milk Butter Cake

PREP TIME: 15 minutes | **COOK TIME:** 40 minutes

MAKES 16 SERVINGS

2¼ cups flour
1 tablespoon baking powder
½ teaspoon salt
1 cup (2 sticks) butter
1 cup milk

1 tablespoon **McCormick®
    Pure Vanilla Extract**
4 eggs
2 cups sugar

PREHEAT oven to 350°F. Grease and flour 13×9-inch baking pan. Mix flour, baking powder and salt in medium bowl. Set aside. Microwave butter and milk in medium microwavable bowl on HIGH 2 minutes or until butter is melted. Stir in vanilla. Set aside.

BEAT eggs in large bowl with electric mixer on medium speed 5 minutes or until fluffy. Gradually add sugar; beat well. Alternately add dry ingredients and milk mixture, beating on low speed after each addition just until mixed. Pour into prepared pan.

BAKE 35 to 40 minutes or until toothpick inserted into center comes out clean. Cool in pan on wire rack. Sprinkle with confectioners' sugar, if desired.

Hummingbird Cake

Cake

- 1 package (2-layer size) yellow cake mix
- 2 ripe bananas, mashed
- 1 can (8 ounces) crushed pineapple, undrained
- 4 eggs
- 1 tablespoon **McCormick® Ground Cinnamon**
- 2 teaspoons **McCormick® Pure Vanilla Extract**
- ½ teaspoon **McCormick® Pure Lemon Extract**

Frosting

- 1 package (8 ounces) cream cheese, softened
- ½ cup (1 stick) butter, softened
- 2 teaspoons **McCormick® Pure Vanilla Extract**
- 1 package (16 ounces) confectioners' sugar
- 1 to 2 tablespoons milk
- ½ teaspoon **McCormick® Color from Nature™- Sunflower**
- ½ cup chopped pecans

PREHEAT oven to 350°F. For the Cake, beat all cake ingredients in large bowl with electric mixer on low speed 30 seconds or until just moistened, scraping sides of bowl occasionally. Beat on medium speed 2 minutes. Pour batter into 2 greased (9-inch) round cake pans.

BAKE 25 to 30 minutes or until toothpick inserted in center comes out clean. Cool in pan 10 minutes; invert cakes onto wire racks. Turn layers right side up and cool completely.

FOR the Frosting, beat cream cheese, butter and vanilla in large bowl on medium speed until light and fluffy. Gradually beat in confectioners' sugar until smooth. Beat in milk, a little at a time, until desired consistency. Stir in yellow food color until evenly blended. Mix 1 cup of the frosting and pecans in another bowl until well blended. Set aside.

PLACE one cooled cake layer on serving platter. Spread pecan frosting evenly on top of first cake layer. Top with second cake layer. Frost top and side of cake with remaining cream cheese frosting. Decorate as desired.

No Bake Vanilla Cheesecake

🕐 **PREP TIME:** 15 minutes

MAKES 8 SERVINGS

2 packages (8 ounces *each*)
  cream cheese, softened

½ cup sugar

1 tablespoon **McCormick®
  Pure Vanilla Extract**

1 tub (8 ounces) frozen
  whipped topping, thawed

1 prepared graham cracker or
  vanilla crumb crust
  (6 ounces)

BEAT cream cheese, sugar and vanilla in large bowl with electric mixer until well blended and smooth.

GENTLY stir in whipped topping. Spoon into crust.

REFRIGERATE 3 hours or until set. Garnish with fresh strawberries or serve with Easy Strawberry Sauce (recipe follows), if desired. Store leftover cheesecake in refrigerator.

Easy Strawberry Sauce: Mix ½ cup strawberry jam with ¼ teaspoon **McCormick® Pure Vanilla Extract**. Prepare cheesecake filling as directed.

Variation: Use 12 graham cracker mini tart crusts in place of the crumb crust. Fill each with ⅓ cup filling. Refrigerate 3 hours or until set. Makes 12 servings.

Red Velvet Cake with Vanilla Cream Cheese Frosting

🕐 **PREP TIME:** 20 minutes │ **COOK TIME:** 40 minutes

MAKES 16 SERVINGS

Red Velvet Cake

- 2½ cups flour
- ½ cup unsweetened cocoa powder
- 1 teaspoon baking soda
- ½ teaspoon salt
- 1 cup (2 sticks) butter, softened
- 2 cups granulated sugar
- 4 eggs
- 1 cup sour cream
- ½ cup milk
- 1 bottle (1 ounce) **McCormick® Red Food Color**
- 2 teaspoons **McCormick® Pure Vanilla Extract**

Vanilla Cream Cheese Frosting

- 1 package (8 ounces) cream cheese, softened
- ¼ cup (½ stick) butter, softened
- 2 tablespoons sour cream
- 2 teaspoons **McCormick® Pure Vanilla Extract**
- 1 package (16 ounces) confectioners' sugar

PREHEAT oven to 350°F. For the Cake, grease and flour 2 (9-inch) round cake pans. Sift flour, cocoa powder, baking soda and salt. Set aside.

BEAT butter and granulated sugar in large bowl with electric mixer on medium speed 5 minutes or until light and fluffy. Beat in eggs, 1 at a time. Mix in sour cream, milk, food color and vanilla. Gradually beat in flour mixture on low speed until just blended. Do not overbeat. Pour batter into prepared pans.

BAKE 35 to 40 minutes or until toothpick inserted in center comes out clean. Cool in pan 10 minutes. Remove from pans; cool completely on wire rack.

FOR the Vanilla Cream Cheese Frosting, beat cream cheese, butter, sour cream and vanilla in large bowl until light and fluffy. Gradually beat in confectioners' sugar until smooth. Fill and frost cooled cake with Frosting.

Variation: Substitute a greased and floured 12-cup bundt pan for the 9-inch cake pans. Bake about 50 minutes. Or, substitute a greased and floured 13×9-inch baking pan; bake about 40 minutes.

PERFECT
Pies & Desserts

Vanilla Pecan Pie

🕐 **PREP TIME:** 15 minutes | **COOK TIME:** 55 minutes

MAKES 10 SERVINGS

1 refrigerated pie crust (from 14.1-ounce package)

1 package (8 ounces) cream cheese, softened

3 eggs, divided

¾ cup sugar, divided

4 teaspoons **McCormick® Pure Vanilla Extract**, divided

½ cup light corn syrup

3 tablespoons butter, melted

¼ teaspoon salt

2 cups pecan pieces, toasted

PREHEAT oven to 350°F. Prepare crust as directed on package for one-crust pie using 9-inch deep dish pie plate. Beat cream cheese, 1 of the eggs, ¼ cup of the sugar and 2 teaspoons of the vanilla in large bowl with electric mixer on medium speed until well blended and smooth. Spread evenly on bottom of crust. Bake 15 minutes.

BEAT remaining 2 eggs and ½ cup sugar in large bowl with wire whisk until smooth. Add corn syrup, butter, remaining 2 teaspoons vanilla and salt; stir until well blended. Sprinkle pecans evenly over baked cream cheese layer. Slowly pour corn syrup mixture over nuts.

BAKE 35 to 40 minutes or until just set in center. Cool completely on wire rack.

S'mores Pie

Graham Cracker Crust

- 1½ cups graham cracker crumbs
- 7 tablespoons butter, melted
- ⅓ cup sugar

Filling

- ¾ cup heavy cream
- 6 ounces semi-sweet chocolate, chopped
- 2 teaspoons **McCormick® Ground Cinnamon**
- 1 tablespoon plus 1 teaspoon **McCormick® Pure Vanilla Extract**, divided
- 1 jar (7 ounces) marshmallow creme
- 4 ounces (½ package) cream cheese, softened
- 1 tub (8 ounces) frozen whipped topping, thawed

MIX all crust ingredients in medium bowl. Press into bottom and up sides of 9-inch pie plate. Set aside.

BRING cream just to boil in small saucepan. Pour over chocolate in medium heatproof bowl. Let stand 1 minute then stir until smooth. Stir in cinnamon and 1 teaspoon of the vanilla. Pour into prepared crust. Refrigerate 30 minutes or until chocolate is firm. (Freeze 15 minutes for faster chilling.)

BEAT marshmallow creme, cream cheese and remaining 1 tablespoon vanilla in large bowl with electric mixer on medium speed until well blended. Gently stir in whipped topping until well blended. Spread evenly over chocolate layer in crust.

REFRIGERATE at least 2 hours or until ready to serve. Garnish with chocolate curls or toasted marshmallows, if desired.

Vanilla Cardamom Whoopie Pies

PREP TIME: 30 minutes | **COOK TIME:** 8 minutes

MAKES 24 SERVINGS

Cookies

- 2 cups flour
- ½ cup unsweetened cocoa powder
- 1¼ teaspoons baking soda
- 1 teaspoon salt
- ¼ teaspoon **McCormick Gourmet™ Organic Ground Cardamom**
- 1 cup buttermilk
- 1 teaspoon **McCormick® Pure Vanilla Extract**
- ½ cup (1 stick) butter, softened
- 1 cup firmly packed brown sugar
- 1 egg

Vanilla Cardamom Filling

- ½ cup (1 stick) butter, softened
- 1½ cups confectioners' sugar
- 1½ cups marshmallow creme
- 2 teaspoons **McCormick Pure Vanilla Extract**
- ¼ teaspoon **McCormick Gourmet™ Organic Ground Cardamom**
- ⅓ cup finely chopped salted shelled pistachios

PREHEAT oven to 350°F. Mix flour, cocoa powder, baking soda, salt and cardamom in medium bowl; set aside. Mix buttermilk and vanilla in small bowl.

BEAT butter and brown sugar in large bowl with electric mixer on medium-high speed until light and fluffy. Add egg; mix well. Add flour mixture alternately with buttermilk mixture, beating on low speed after each addition until smooth and scraping down sides of bowl occasionally. Spoon 1 tablespoon of batter, 2 inches apart, onto parchment paper-lined large baking sheets. (Cookies will spread so avoid crowding them on baking sheet.

BAKE 8 minutes or until cookies are puffed and spring back when touched, turning baking sheets halfway through baking. Cool on baking sheets 1 minute. Remove to wire racks; cool completely.

FOR the Vanilla Cardamom Filling, beat butter, confectioners' sugar, marshmallow creme, vanilla and cardamom in medium bowl with electric mixer on medium speed until light and fluffy.

TO assemble the Whoopie Pies, place 1 tablespoon filling on flat side of 1 cookie. Top with a second cookie, pressing gently to spread the filling. Repeat with remaining cookies. Roll edge of cookies in chopped pistachios. Store whoopie pies between layers of wax paper in airtight container in refrigerator up to 5 days.

Signature Pumpkin Pie

🕐 **PREP TIME:** 5 minutes | **COOK TIME:** 55 minutes

MAKES 8 SERVINGS

1 frozen unbaked deep dish pie crust, 9-inch
1 can (15 ounces) pumpkin
1 can (14 ounces) sweetened condensed milk

2 eggs
1 teaspoon **McCormick® Pure Vanilla Extract**
1 tablespoon **McCormick® Pumpkin Pie Spice**

PREHEAT oven to 425°F. Place pie crust on large foil-lined baking sheet.

MIX pumpkin, milk, eggs, vanilla and pumpkin pie spice in large bowl until smooth. Pour into crust.

BAKE 15 minutes. Reduce oven temperature to 350°F. Bake 40 minutes longer or until knife inserted 1 inch from crust comes out clean. Cool completely on wire rack. Serve with Vanilla Whipped Cream, if desired.

Test Kitchen Tip: Place the frozen pie crust in its pie pan on a baking sheet before pouring in the pumpkin filling. This is to catch any spills while transporting to the oven or while baking.

Substitution Tip: Use 1½ teaspoons **McCormick® Ground Cinnamon**, ¾ teaspoon **McCormick® Ground Ginger**, ¼ teaspoon **McCormick® Ground Nutmeg** and ⅛ teaspoon **McCormick® Ground Cloves** in place of the Pumpkin Pie Spice.

Vanilla Whipped Cream

🕐 **PREP TIME:** 5 minutes

1 cup heavy cream
¼ cup confectioners' sugar

1 teaspoon **McCormick® Pure Vanilla Extract**

BEAT cream, confectioners' sugar and vanilla in medium bowl with electric mixer on high speed until stiff peaks form. Cover.

REFRIGERATE until ready to serve.

Vanilla Crème Brûlée

🕐 **PREP TIME:** 10 minutes | **COOK TIME:** 40 minutes

MAKES 8 SERVINGS

Butter, for coating
3 cups heavy cream
1 tablespoon **McCormick®
   Pure Vanilla Extract**

6 egg yolks
¾ cup sugar, divided

PREHEAT oven to 325°F. Lightly coat 8 (4-ounce) ramekins or shallow fluted dishes with butter. Place in shallow roasting pan.

BRING cream to simmer in medium saucepan on medium heat. Remove from heat. Stir in vanilla. Beat egg yolks and ½ cup of the sugar in large bowl with wire whisk until pale yellow. Gradually whisk in cream mixture. Pour into ramekins. Carefully pour enough hot water into roasting pan to come halfway up sides of ramekins.

BAKE 25 to 30 minutes or until custards are almost set in center. Cool custards in water bath. Remove from water bath. Cover each custard with plastic wrap. Refrigerate at least 4 hours or overnight.

SPRINKLE 1½ teaspoons of the remaining sugar evenly over each custard. Holding a hand-held torch 4 inches from the sugar, lightly brown the sugar using a slow even motion. Remove the flame just before desired degree of browning is reached, as the sugar will continue to brown for a few seconds.

REFRIGERATE 30 minutes before serving to allow topping to harden.

Test Kitchen Tip: Sugar topping can also be browned under a broiler. Place custards on a baking sheet. Broil 6 inches from heat for 4 to 6 minutes or until sugar is melted and golden brown.

Easier than Apple Pie

PREP TIME: 15 minutes | **COOK TIME:** 20 minutes

MAKES 8 SERVINGS

1 refrigerated pie crust (from 14.1-ounce package dough)

1 egg white, lightly beaten

¾ cup plus 1 teaspoon sugar, divided

2 tablespoons cornstarch

2 teaspoons **McCormick® Ground Cinnamon**

4 cups tart apples, such as Granny Smith or Braeburn, thinly sliced (about 4 cups)

PREHEAT oven to 425°F. Unroll crust. Place on foil-lined 12-inch pizza pan. If necessary, press out any folds or creases. Brush crust with about ½ of the beaten egg white.

MIX ¾ cup sugar, cornstarch and cinnamon in medium bowl. Toss with apples. Spoon into center of crust, spreading to within 2 inches of edges. Fold 2-inch edge of crust up over apples, pleating or folding crust as needed. Brush crust with remaining egg white; sprinkle with remaining 1 teaspoon sugar.

BAKE 20 minutes or until apples are tender. Cool slightly before serving.

Test Kitchen Tip: Try adding ¼ cup raisins, dried cranberries or dried cherries to the fruit mixture.

Spiced Easier than Apple Pie: Prepare as directed. Use 1½ teaspoons **McCormick® Pumpkin Pie Spice** or 1 teaspoon **McCormick® Apple Pie Spice** in place of the cinnamon.

Peppermint Chocolate Lasagna

Brownie

1   package (family-size) fudge brownie mix

Chocolate Mousse

8   ounces bittersweet chocolate, coarsely chopped

2¼   cups heavy cream, divided

1   tablespoon **McCormick® Pure Vanilla Extract**

¼   cup granulated sugar

Peppermint Cream

1½   cups heavy cream

⅓   cup confectioners' sugar

¼   teaspoon **McCormick® Pure Peppermint Extract**

PREPARE brownie mix as directed on package in 13×9-inch baking pan. Cool on wire rack.

FOR the Chocolate Mousse, microwave chocolate in medium microwaveable bowl on HIGH 1 minute; stir. Microwave additional 30 seconds at a time, stirring until chocolate is smooth and melted. Add ¼ cup of the heavy cream; stir until smooth. Stir in vanilla. Let stand 10 minutes to cool slightly. Beat remaining 2 cups heavy cream and granulated sugar in large bowl with electric mixer on medium speed until stiff peaks form. Gently stir in ½ of the chocolate mixture with spatula until well blended. Gently stir in remaining chocolate mixture.

FOR the Peppermint Cream, beat heavy cream, confectioners' sugar and peppermint extract in large bowl with electric mixer on high speed until soft peaks form.

SPREAD ½ of the Peppermint Cream over brownie. Spread evenly with Chocolate Mousse. Top with remaining Peppermint Cream.

Make It Easy: Purchase a prepared brownie instead of making the brownie mix.

SIMPLE
Sides &
Salads

Vanilla Green Beans Amandine

1 pound fresh green beans, trimmed

2 tablespoons butter

1 tablespoon dry white wine

1½ teaspoons **McCormick® Pure Vanilla Extract**

½ teaspoon **McCormick® Onion Powder**

¼ teaspoon salt

⅛ to ¼ teaspoon **McCormick® Coarse Ground Black Pepper**

¼ cup sliced almonds, toasted

PLACE green beans in boiling water to cover in medium saucepan on medium-high heat. Cook 7 to 8 minutes or until tender-crisp. Drain.

MELT butter in same saucepan on low heat. Add wine, vanilla, onion powder, salt and pepper; cook and stir 1 minute. Add green beans; toss to coat well. Sprinkle with almonds.

Test Kitchen Tip: Prepare as directed, using 1 bag (16 ounces) frozen green beans in place of the fresh green beans. Cook as directed on package.

To toast sliced almonds: Spread almonds in single layer on baking sheet. Toast in preheated 350°F oven 3 to 5 minutes or until golden brown.

Gnocchi in Vanilla Brown Butter Sauce with Baby Spinach and Toasted Hazelnuts

🕐 **PREP TIME:** 15 minutes | **COOK TIME:** 15 minutes

MAKES 3 SERVINGS

- 1 package (1 pound) gnocchi
- ¼ cup (½ stick) butter
- 1 teaspoon minced garlic
- 1 teaspoon brown sugar
- ¾ teaspoon **McCormick® Pure Vanilla Extract**
- ½ teaspoon salt
- ¼ teaspoon **McCormick® Rosemary Leaves**
- 2 cups baby spinach leaves
- ¼ cup heavy cream
- ¼ cup toasted chopped hazelnuts

COOK gnocchi as directed on package. Drain well. Meanwhile, melt butter in large skillet on medium heat 4 minutes or until nut brown in color and aroma. Add garlic, brown sugar, vanilla, salt and rosemary; cook and stir 30 seconds or until garlic is fragrant and sugar is dissolved.

STIR in cooked gnocchi and spinach. Cook and stir 1 minute or just until spinach is slightly wilted. Stir in cream and hazelnuts. Serve immediately.

Field Greens with Oranges, Strawberries and Vanilla Vinaigrette

🕐 **PREP TIME:** 20 minutes

MAKES 6 SERVINGS

Vanilla Vinaigrette

- ⅓ cup olive oil
- 3 tablespoons white wine vinegar
- 1 teaspoon **McCormick® Pure Vanilla Extract**
- ½ teaspoon salt
- ½ teaspoon sugar
- ¼ teaspoon **McCormick® Ground Black Pepper**

Salad

- 1 package (6 ounces) field greens or baby spinach leaves
- 2 seedless oranges, peeled and sectioned
- 2 cups strawberry halves or slices
- ½ cup toasted pecan pieces

FOR the Vanilla Viniagrette, mix all ingredients in small bowl with wire whisk until well blended.

TOSS greens with oranges, strawberries and pecans in large bowl. (Or divide among individual serving plates.) Serve with vinaigrette.

Vanilla Glazed Roasted Squash and Apples

PREP TIME: 20 minutes | **COOK TIME:** 45 minutes

MAKES 12 SERVINGS

1 medium butternut squash, (about 1½ pounds), peeled, seeded and cut into 1-inch cubes

1 medium Vidalia onion, cut into thin wedges (1 cup)

¼ cup (½ stick) butter, melted

¼ cup firmly packed light brown sugar

1 tablespoon **McCormick® Pure Vanilla Extract**

1 teaspoon salt

½ to 1 teaspoon **McCormick® Ground Nutmeg**

½ teaspoon **McCormick® Ground Black Pepper**

2 unpeeled apples, cored and cut into ½-inch-thick wedges

PREHEAT oven to 450°F. Toss squash and onion in large bowl.

MIX butter, brown sugar, vanilla, salt, nutmeg and pepper in small bowl until well blended. Pour over squash mixture; toss to coat well. Arrange in single layer on foil-lined large shallow baking pan.

BAKE 15 minutes. Add apples; toss to mix well. Bake 25 to 30 minutes longer or until squash and apples are tender.

Test Kitchen Tip: Use crisp sweet-tart apples, such as Braeburn, Empire or Jonagold.

Vanilla Shrimp Crostini

PREP TIME: 15 minutes | **COOK TIME:** 10 minutes

MAKES 24 SERVINGS

1 loaf French bread

2 ounces Gruyère or Manchego cheese

4 tablespoons butter, divided

1 pound raw large shrimp, peeled and deveined

½ cup dry white wine

2 teaspoons **McCormick® Pure Vanilla Extract**

½ teaspoon **McCormick® Basil Leaves**

¼ teaspoon **McCormick® Ground Red Pepper**

SLICE bread on the diagonal into 24 (½-inch-thick) slices. Place on baking sheet; broil until lightly toasted on both sides. Using a vegetable peeler, shave cheese into very thin slices. Set aside.

HEAT 2 tablespoons of the butter in large skillet on medium-high heat. Add shrimp; cook and stir 2 minutes or just until shrimp turn pink. Add wine, vanilla, basil and red pepper; cook 2 to 4 minutes. Remove shrimp from pan. Boil sauce 1 minute; remove pan from heat and whisk in remaining butter, 1 tablespoon at a time. The butter must melt gradually to form a creamy sauce.

TO assemble appetizers, brush toasted bread slices with warm sauce from skillet. Top with 1 to 2 thin slices of cheese, then 1 to 2 shrimp (depending on size); brush with additional sauce.

Test Kitchen Tip: If desired, add chopped roasted red peppers and chopped chives, for garnish.

Shaved Brussels Sprouts Salad with Cranberries and Toasted Walnuts

🕐 **PREP TIME:** 15 minutes

MAKES 5 SERVINGS

- ⅓ cup olive oil
- 3 tablespoons Champagne vinegar
- ½ teaspoon **McCormick® Pure Vanilla Extract**
- ½ teaspoon **McCormick® Rubbed Sage**
- ½ teaspoon salt
- ½ teaspoon sugar
- ¼ teaspoon **McCormick® Coarse Ground Black Pepper**
- ½ cup dried cranberries
- 12 ounces fresh Brussels sprouts, trimmed and thinly sliced
- ¼ cup chopped walnuts, toasted

MIX oil, vinegar, vanilla and seasonings in small bowl with wire whisk until well blended. Add cranberries; let stand 30 minutes to allow cranberries to soften.

TOSS Brussels sprouts and walnuts in large bowl until well blended. Drizzle with dressing; toss to coat well. Serve immediately.

Ginger Spiced Mashed Sweet Potatoes

🕐 **PREP TIME:** 5 minutes

MAKES 4 SERVINGS

2 pounds sweet potatoes

2 tablespoons butter, softened

2 teaspoons **McCormick® Pure Vanilla Extract**

1 teaspoon **McCormick® Ground Ginger**

¼ teaspoon **Sea Salt from McCormick® Sea Salt Grinder**

¼ teaspoon **McCormick® Thyme Leaves**

PIERCE each sweet potato twice with fork so excess steam can escape while cooking. Microwave on HIGH 5 to 10 minutes or until tender, turning over halfway through cooking. Let stand 5 minutes or until cool enough to handle. Remove skin from the sweet potatoes.

PLACE sweet potatoes and remaining ingredients in large bowl. Mash until smooth and well blended. Serve immediately.

To Boil Sweet Potatoes: Peel and cut sweet potatoes into 2-inch chunks. Place in large saucepan. Add cold water to cover 1 inch over sweet potatoes. Bring to boil; cover. Cook on medium-low heat 20 to 30 minutes or until tender. Drain.

Vanilla Summertime Slaw

🕐 **PREP TIME:** 10 minutes

MAKES 6 SERVINGS

1 cup mayonnaise

2 tablespoons sugar

2 tablespoons vinegar

1 teaspoon **McCormick® Celery Seed**

1 teaspoon **McCormick® Ground Mustard**

1 teaspoon **Lawry's® Seasoned Salt**

½ teaspoon **McCormick® Pure Vanilla Extract**

1 package (16 ounces) shredded coleslaw mix

MIX mayonnaise, sugar, vinegar, celery seed, ground mustard, seasoned salt and vanilla in large bowl. Add coleslaw mix; toss to coat well. Cover.

REFRIGERATE 2 hours or until ready to serve. Stir before serving.

SENSATIONAL
Sweets &
Treats

Pumpkin Bread Pudding with Vanilla Butter Sauce

PREP TIME: 15 minutes | **COOK TIME:** 45 minutes

MAKES 16 SERVINGS

Pumpkin Bread Pudding

- 2½ cups milk
- ¾ cup sugar
- 6 ounces white baking chocolate, cut into chunks
- ¼ cup (½ stick) butter
- 4 eggs
- 1 can (15 ounces) pumpkin
- 1 tablespoon **McCormick® Pumpkin Pie Spice**
- 1 teaspoon **McCormick® Pure Vanilla Extract**
- 8 cups cubed Italian bread
- 1 cup dried cherries
- 1 cup chopped pecans, divided

Vanilla Butter Sauce

- ½ cup heavy cream
- ½ cup sugar
- 2 tablespoons butter
- ½ teaspoon **McCormick® Pumpkin Pie Spice**
- 1 teaspoon **McCormick® Pure Vanilla Extract**

PREHEAT oven to 325°F. For the Pumpkin Bread Pudding, mix milk, sugar, white chocolate and butter in large microwavable bowl. Microwave on HIGH 4 minutes or until butter is melted, stirring after 2 minutes. Stir until white chocolate is completely melted. Set aside.

BEAT eggs, pumpkin, pumpkin pie spice and vanilla in large bowl until well blended. Add white chocolate mixture; stir until well blended. Add bread cubes, cherries and ½ cup of the pecans; stir until well coated. Spread evenly in greased 13×9-inch baking dish. Sprinkle with remaining pecans.

BAKE 40 to 45 minutes or until knife inserted in center comes out clean.

FOR the Vanilla Butter Sauce, mix cream, sugar, butter and pumpkin pie spice in medium saucepan. Bring to boil on medium heat. Reduce heat to low; simmer 5 to 10 minutes or until slightly thickened. Remove from heat. Stir in vanilla extract. Serve warm with Pumpkin Bread Pudding.

Homemade Cranberry Sauce

PREP TIME: 5 minutes | COOK TIME: 15 minutes

MAKES 2 CUPS

1 cup sugar

1 cup water

1 package (12 ounces) fresh cranberries, rinsed and drained

½ teaspoon **McCormick® Ground Cinnamon**

½ teaspoon grated orange peel (optional)

½ teaspoon **McCormick® Pure Vanilla Extract**

MIX sugar and water in medium saucepan. Bring to boil on medium-high heat. Add cranberries, cinnamon and orange peel, if desired; return to boil. Reduce heat to medium-low; simmer 10 minutes or until cranberries burst and sauce begins to thicken, stirring occasionally.

REMOVE from heat. Stir in vanilla. Cool to room temperature. Cover.

REFRIGERATE until ready to serve.

Make Ahead: Cranberry sauce can be prepared up to 1 week ahead. Store in refrigerator. Stir before serving.

Test Kitchen Tip: Use ¼ teaspoon **McCormick® Pure Orange Extract** in place of orange peel.

Classic Eggnog

PREP TIME: 10 minutes | **COOK TIME:** 10 minutes

MAKES 10 SERVINGS

3 cups milk

1 cup light cream

3 **McCormick® Whole Cloves**

2 sticks **McCormick® Cinnamon Sticks**

4 teaspoons **McCormick® Pure Vanilla Extract**

½ teaspoon **McCormick® Ground Nutmeg**

6 egg yolks

¾ cup sugar

BRING milk, cream, whole cloves, cinnamon sticks, vanilla and nutmeg just to boil in medium saucepan on low heat. Beat egg yolks and sugar in medium bowl until pale yellow in color and fluffy. Gradually add 1 cup of the hot milk mixture, mixing with wire whisk until well blended. Gradually whisk mixture back into the remaining milk mixture in the saucepan. Cook and stir on medium-low heat 3 to 5 minutes or until mixture thickens and coats the back of a spoon.

STRAIN into large bowl. Cool slightly. Cover.

REFRIGERATE overnight or until well chilled.

Variation:

Coconut Milk Eggnog: Use 1 can (13.66 ounces) Thai Kitchen® Coconut Milk in place of the light cream.

Easy Green Velvet Cupcakes

PREP TIME: 20 minutes | **COOK TIME:** 20 minutes

MAKES 24 SERVINGS

1 package (2-layer size) German chocolate cake mix with pudding

1 cup sour cream

½ cup water

¼ cup unsweetened cocoa powder

¼ cup vegetable oil

1 bottle **McCormick® Green Food Color**

3 eggs

2 teaspoons **McCormick® Pure Vanilla Extract**

Vanilla Cream Cheese Frosting (recipe follows)

Green sprinkles

PREHEAT oven to 350°F. Beat cake mix, sour cream, water, cocoa powder, oil, food color, eggs and vanilla in large bowl with electric mixer on low speed just until moistened, scraping sides of bowl frequently. Beat on medium speed 2 minutes.

POUR batter into 24 paper-lined muffin cups, filling each cup ⅔ full.

BAKE 20 minutes or until toothpick inserted in center of cupcake comes out clean. Cool in pan 10 minutes. Remove from pans; cool completely on wire rack. Frost with Vanilla Cream Cheese Frosting. Decorate with sprinkles.

Vanilla Cream Cheese Frosting: Beat 1 package (8 ounces) cream cheese, softened, ¼ cup (½ stick) butter, softened, 2 tablespoons sour cream and 2 teaspoons **McCormick® Pure Vanilla Extract** in large bowl until light and fluffy. Gradually beat in 1 package (16 ounces) confectioners' sugar until smooth. Makes 2½ cups.

Variation:

Minty Green Cream Cheese Frosting: Stir ½ teaspoon **McCormick® Pure Peppermint Extract** and ½ teaspoon **McCormick® Green Food Color** into Vanilla Cream Cheese Frosting.

Pumpkin Pie Layered Cheesecake

PREP TIME: 20 minutes | **COOK TIME:** 50 minutes

MAKES 12 SERVINGS

Graham Cracker Crust

- 1½ cups graham cracker crumbs
- ⅓ cup butter, melted
- 2 tablespoons sugar
- 2 teaspoons **McCormick® Pumpkin Pie Spice**

Cheesecake Filling

- 3 packages (8 ounces *each*) cream cheese, softened
- 1 cup sugar
- 4 eggs
- 1 cup sour cream
- 1 can (15 ounces) pumpkin
- ¼ cup flour
- 1 tablespoon **McCormick® Pumpkin Pie Spice**
- 2 teaspoons **McCormick® Pure Vanilla Extract**

PREHEAT oven to 325°F. For the Crust, mix all ingredients in medium bowl. Press evenly onto bottom and up sides of 9-inch springform pan.

FOR the Cheesecake Filling, beat cream cheese and sugar in large bowl with electric mixer on medium speed until fluffy. Add eggs, 1 at a time, mixing on low speed after each addition just until blended. Add sour cream; mix well. Remove 1 cup batter to medium bowl; beat in pumpkin, flour and pumpkin pie spice until smooth. Stir vanilla into remaining plain batter. Pour ½ of the vanilla batter into crust. Gently pour pumpkin batter over top. Top with remaining vanilla batter.

BAKE 50 minutes or until center is almost set. Turn off oven; let cheesecake stand in oven 2 hours or until cooled. Remove from oven.

REFRIGERATE 4 hours or overnight. Run small knife around sides of pan to loosen crust; remove sides of pan. Store leftover cheesecake in refrigerator.

Vanilla Cardamom Fizztini

Vanilla Cardamom Syrup

1½   cups water

¾   cup sugar

3   tablespoons fresh Meyer
     lemon juice

6   **McCormick Gourmet™
     Whole Cardamom Pods**

1   teaspoon **McCormick® Pure
     Vanilla Extract**

For each Fizztini

¾   cup cold seltzer

2   tablespoons Vanilla
     Cardamom Syrup

     Sugar in the Raw®

FOR the Vanilla Cardamom Syrup, mix water, sugar, lemon juice and cardamom pods in small saucepan. Bring to boil. Reduce heat to low; simmer 10 minutes or until sugar is completely dissolved. Remove from heat. Let stand 1 hour. Stir in vanilla. Strain syrup through cheesecloth. Cover and refrigerate until ready to use. This makes enough syrup for 15 Fizztinis.

FOR each Fizztini, coat rim of martini glass lightly with Vanilla Cardamom Syrup. Dip rim of glass into Sugar in the Raw to coat. Mix seltzer and syrup. Pour into martini glass.

Caramel Pumpkin Oatmeal Bars

PREP TIME: 15 minutes | **COOK TIME:** 35 minutes

MAKES 24 SERVINGS

2 cups flour
2 cups old fashioned oats
1½ cups firmly packed light brown sugar
1 teaspoon baking soda
½ teaspoon salt
1½ teaspoons **McCormick® Ground Cinnamon**
¾ teaspoon **McCormick® Ground Ginger**

¼ teaspoon **McCormick® Ground Nutmeg**
1 cup (2 stick) butter, melted
1 cup canned pumpkin
1 teaspoon **McCormick® Pure Vanilla Extract**
7 ounces caramels, unwrapped
2 tablespoons milk

PREHEAT oven to 350°F. Mix flour, oats, brown sugar, baking soda, salt and spices in large bowl. Add butter; stir until mixture is well blended and forms coarse crumbs. Reserve ½ (about 2¼ cups) for the topping. Add pumpkin and vanilla to remaining mixture in bowl; stir until well blended. Press evenly into bottom of greased foil-lined 13×9-inch baking pan. Set aside.

MICROWAVE caramels and milk in medium microwavable bowl on HIGH 2 to 3 minutes or until caramels are completely melted, stirring after every minute. Let stand 1 minute. Pour over pumpkin mixture in pan, spreading to within ½ inch of edges. Sprinkle with reserved crumb mixture.

BAKE 30 to 35 minutes or until light golden brown. Cool in pan on wire rack. Lift from pan. Cut into bars.

Test Kitchen Tip: Prepare as directed, using 1 tablespoon **McCormick® Pumpkin Pie Spice** in place of the cinnamon, ginger and nutmeg.

Red Velvet Mug Cake with Pecans and Cream Cheese Frosting

🕐 **PREP TIME:** 5 minutes | **COOK TIME:** 2 minutes

MAKES 1 MUG

Red Velvet Mug Cake with Pecans

- 2 tablespoons semi-sweet chocolate chips
- 1 tablespoon butter
- 2 tablespoons packed brown sugar
- 2 tablespoons whipped cream cheese
- 2 tablespoons flour
- 1 egg yolk
- 1 teaspoon **McCormick® Pure Vanilla Extract**
- ½ teaspoon **McCormick® Red Food Color**
- 2 tablespoons chopped pecans

Cream Cheese Frosting

- 1 tablespoon whipped cream cheese
- 1 teaspoon granulated sugar
- 1 teaspoon milk

FOR the Red Velvet Mug Cake, microwave chocolate chips and butter in microwavable coffee mug on HIGH 30 seconds or until melted. Stir. Add remaining ingredients except pecans; mix well. Gently stir in pecans.

MICROWAVE on HIGH 45 seconds to 1 minute or until center looks almost set. Let stand 5 minutes before serving.

FOR the Cream Cheese Frosting, mix cream cheese and granulated sugar in small bowl until well blended. Stir in milk. Drizzle over mug cake.

Caution: Mug may be hot. Use pot holders when removing from microwave.

To Make Multiple Batches: Prepare up to 4 Red Velvet Mug Cakes in the microwave at a time.

Carrot Cake Swirled Cheesecake Bars

🕐 **PREP TIME:** 15 minutes │ **COOK TIME:** 40 minutes

MAKES 24 SERVINGS

1 cup plus 2 tablespoons flour, divided	4 eggs, divided
2 cups sugar, divided	2 teaspoons **McCormick® Pure Vanilla Extract**
1½ teaspoons **McCormick® Ground Cinnamon**	1½ cups finely grated carrots
1 teaspoon baking soda	3 packages (8 ounces *each*) cream cheese, softened
½ teaspoon **McCormick® Ground Nutmeg**	¼ cup milk
¼ teaspoon salt	1 teaspoon **McCormick® Pure Lemon Extract**
⅔ cup vegetable oil	

PREHEAT oven to 325°F. Mix 1 cup *each* of the flour and sugar, cinnamon and baking soda, nutmeg and salt in large bowl. Add oil, 2 of the eggs, vanilla and carrots; mix well. Spread ½ of the batter into greased and floured 13×9-inch baking pan. Reserve remaining batter. Set aside.

BEAT cream cheese and remaining 1 cup sugar in another large bowl with electric mixer on medium speed until well blended. Add milk, remaining 2 tablespoons flour and lemon extract; beat until well blended. Add remaining 2 eggs, 1 at a time, beating on low speed after each addition just until blended.

DROP spoonfuls of the cream cheese mixture and reserved carrot cake batter, alternately, over the carrot cake batter in pan. Cut through several times with knife for marble effect.

BAKE 40 minutes or until toothpick inserted in center comes out clean. Cool in pan on wire rack.

Candy Corn Fudge

🕐 **PREP TIME:** 15 minutes

MAKES 36 SERVINGS

2 pounds white baking chocolate, chopped

1 can (14 ounces) sweetened condensed milk

1 tablespoon **McCormick® Pure Vanilla Extract**

½ teaspoon plus ⅛ teaspoon Sunflower color from **McCormick® Color from Nature™-Assorted Food Color**, divided

⅛ teaspoon Berry color from **McCormick® Color from Nature™-Assorted Food Color**

MIX chocolate and sweetened condensed milk in large microwavable bowl. Microwave on HIGH 2 to 3 minutes or until chocolate is almost melted, stirring after each minute. Stir again until chocolate is completely melted. Stir in vanilla.

DIVIDE fudge mixture evenly into 3 bowls. Stir ⅛ teaspoon of the Sunflower color into first bowl. Stir ½ teaspoon of the Sunflower color and ⅛ teaspoon of the Berry color into second bowl. Leave third bowl untinted.

POUR the yellow fudge mixture evenly into foil-lined 9×5-inch loaf pan. Layer with the orange and white fudge mixtures.

REFRIGERATE 2 hours or until firm. Use foil to lift out of pan onto cutting board. Cut into small triangles to serve. Store in tightly covered container at cool room temperature.

No Bake Cookie Dough Ice Cream Sandwich

🕐 **PREP TIME:** 20 minutes

MAKES 16 SERVINGS

½ cup creamy peanut butter

⅓ cup butter, softened

⅔ cup confectioners' sugar

⅓ cup firmly packed brown sugar

2 teaspoons **McCormick® Pure Vanilla Extract**

1¼ cups vanilla wafer crumbs (about 35 vanilla wafers)

1 cup miniature chocolate chips

4 cups vanilla ice cream, softened

MIX peanut butter and butter in large bowl until well blended. Add sugars and vanilla; stir until blended and smooth. Stir in vanilla wafer crumbs and chocolate chips.

LINE 8-inch square pan with foil, with ends of foil extending over sides of pan. Press ½ of the dough into an even layer in pan. Pat remaining dough on parchment or wax paper into 8-inch square. Gently spread ice cream over layer in pan. Flip 8-inch square layer onto top of ice cream. Peel back parchment paper. Cover with foil.

FREEZE 3 hours or until firm. Let stand at room temperature 2 to 3 minutes to allow ice cream to soften slightly. Cut into 16 bars. Wrap each in plastic wrap. Store in freezer.

Test Kitchen Tips:

• Dip knife in hot water before cutting dessert into bars.

• To make a nut-free cookie dough, replace the peanut butter with ½ cup marshmallow creme.

Spiced Caramel Apple Cider

🕒 **PREP TIME:** 5 minutes

MAKES 4 SERVINGS

4 cups apple cider	2 teaspoons **McCormick®**
¼ cup caramel topping	**Pure Vanilla Extract**
1 teaspoon **McCormick® Apple Pie Spice**	

BRING apple cider, caramel topping and apple pie spice to simmer in medium saucepan. Stir in vanilla.

POUR into serving cups. Serve topped with whipped cream, additional caramel topping and apple pie spice, if desired.

Flavor Variations:

Reduce vanilla to 1 teaspoon and add the following extracts:

Spiced Caramel Orange Cider: Use ¼ teaspoon **McCormick® Pure Orange Extract**.

Spiced Caramel Maple Cider: Use ¾ teaspoon **McCormick® Maple Extract**.

Spiced Caramel Rum Cider:
Use ¾ teaspoon **McCormick® Rum Extract**.

Index

Metric Conversion Chart

VOLUME MEASUREMENTS (dry)

$^1/_8$ teaspoon = 0.5 mL
$^1/_4$ teaspoon = 1 mL
$^1/_2$ teaspoon = 2 mL
$^3/_4$ teaspoon = 4 mL
1 teaspoon = 5 mL
1 tablespoon = 15 mL
2 tablespoons = 30 mL
$^1/_4$ cup = 60 mL
$^1/_3$ cup = 75 mL
$^1/_2$ cup = 125 mL
$^2/_3$ cup = 150 mL
$^3/_4$ cup = 175 mL
1 cup = 250 mL
2 cups = 1 pint = 500 mL
3 cups = 750 mL
4 cups = 1 quart = 1 L

VOLUME MEASUREMENTS (fluid)

1 fluid ounce (2 tablespoons) = 30 mL
4 fluid ounces ($^1/_2$ cup) = 125 mL
8 fluid ounces (1 cup) = 250 mL
12 fluid ounces (1$^1/_2$ cups) = 375 mL
16 fluid ounces (2 cups) = 500 mL

WEIGHTS (mass)

$^1/_2$ ounce = 15 g
1 ounce = 30 g
3 ounces = 90 g
4 ounces = 120 g
8 ounces = 225 g
10 ounces = 285 g
12 ounces = 360 g
16 ounces = 1 pound = 450 g

DIMENSIONS

$^1/_{16}$ inch = 2 mm
$^1/_8$ inch = 3 mm
$^1/_4$ inch = 6 mm
$^1/_2$ inch = 1.5 cm
$^3/_4$ inch = 2 cm
1 inch = 2.5 cm

OVEN TEMPERATURES

250°F = 120°C
275°F = 140°C
300°F = 150°C
325°F = 160°C
350°F = 180°C
375°F = 190°C
400°F = 200°C
425°F = 220°C
450°F = 230°C

BAKING PAN SIZES

Utensil	Size in Inches/Quarts	Metric Volume	Size in Centimeters
Baking or	8×8×2	2 L	20×20×5
Cake Pan	9×9×2	2.5 L	23×23×5
(square or	12×8×2	3 L	30×20×5
rectangular)	13×9×2	3.5 L	33×23×5
Loaf Pan	8×4×3	1.5 L	20×10×7
	9×5×3	2 L	23×13×7
Round Layer	8×1½	1.2 L	20×4
Cake Pan	9×1½	1.5 L	23×4
Pie Plate	8×1¼	750 mL	20×3
	9×1¼	1 L	23×3
Baking Dish	1 quart	1 L	—
or Casserole	1½ quart	1.5 L	—
	2 quart	2 L	—